Contents

Detroit

Chapter 1

Revealing Heavenly Wonders

The telescope is a wonderful tool that has enabled humanity to unlock many of the secrets of the **universe**. But interest in the sky and the objects that move through it did not begin with this relatively recent invention. Long before people had telescopes, they eagerly studied the great sky-dome that arched above the mountains, plains, and seas. With a sense of wonder, members of Stone Age human tribes watched the daily and monthly journeys of the Sun, Moon, and **stars**. Scientists have found carvings of the Moon's phases on pieces of bone and rock dating back tens of thousands of years.

Many thousands of years passed and humans learned to grow crops and build cities. In a like manner, their observations of the heavens also became more advanced. About 5,000 years ago a people known as the Sumerians rose in the Middle East in what is now Iraq. They erected the world's first observatories to study the heavens. These were high towers called **ziggurats**.

The priests who ran these facilities carefully traced and recorded the movements of the heavenly bodies. The observers could not explain the true nature of these objects. This was largely because they could not see them up close. Later, some ancient Greek thinkers suggested that the objects in the night sky are other suns and earths. Though correct, this was only an educated guess. As long as visions of the heavens were limited to the human eye, the true nature of the universe was destined to remain beyond the understanding of human observers.

This photo shows the remains of a ziggurat towering among the ruins of the Sumerian city of Ur.

Hans Lippershey experiments with his new invention, the spyglass.

The First Telescopes

The abilities of the human eye began to be surpassed in the early 1600s. The earliest known telescope pioneer was a Dutch eyeglass maker named Hans Lippershey. At the time, his craft was already a few centuries old. Sometime in the 1200s, Europeans had begun to use glass lenses that were thicker in the middle than at the edges to help people with poor vision. Eyeglasses made fuzzy images appear sharper. But they did not make the images look larger and closer.

One day Lippershey was tinkering with some of his lenses and noticed something unusual. When he placed one lens in front of another, objects resting just beyond the lenses were magnified slightly. He experimented further and soon built what he called a spyglass. It was the world's first optical telescope. An optical telescope focuses light into the human eye. More specifically, it was the first refracting telescope, or **refractor**, which uses two lenses. The first lens (often called the objective lens) collects and refracts (bends) incoming light, focusing it into a tiny image. The secondary lens, placed

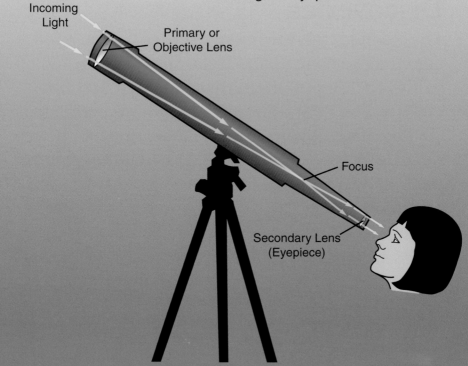

Refracting Telescope

Light entering a refracting telescope is directed through two lenses, one at each end. Focus is achieved by moving the eyepiece lens in or out.

Incoming
Light

Primary or
Objective Lens

Focus

Secondary Lens
(Eyepiece)

directly in front of the first, magnifies the image, making it look larger to the eye.

Lippershey and his friends saw the new invention mainly as a novelty. Soon, well-to-do people in Holland and France were playing with it at parties. They were intrigued by the way it made people and buildings appear closer. Lippershey also realized that his device might have a practical application. Namely, army officers could use it to observe enemy troop movements up close. So in 1608 he presented the spyglass to the Dutch government. Today it seems incredible that at the time neither the inventor nor anyone else thought about using the new invention to study the heavens.

Galileo's Momentous Discoveries

The credit for this revolutionary idea goes to a brilliant Italian scholar named Galileo Galilei. In 1609, while teaching mathematics in Padua, in northern Italy, he heard about Lippershey's spyglass. Galileo had never actually seen one of these devices. But he immediately grasped the principle involved and quickly got to work making his own telescopes. The largest, which was superior to any of Lippershey's spyglasses, magnified 32 times. That is, an object observed with the instrument appeared 32 times closer than it did to the unaided eye.

Galileo was an **astronomer** as well as a mathematician. So he immediately recognized the telescope's potential for revealing the secrets of the heavens. Indeed, the first night he turned his device skyward he could barely contain his excitement. No longer simply points of light in the darkness, Venus, Jupiter, and Mars appeared as globes like the Moon. Clearly they were other **planets**. Meanwhile, the telescope revealed that the Moon itself was covered with craters, mountains, and what appeared to be seas. (Later researchers found that they are not seas but vast plains of dust.)

This is a modern reconstruction of Galileo's first telescope.

Almost every night Galileo made some new discovery. Perhaps his most important finding was of four tiny points of light clustered near Jupiter. Watching them over the course of several nights, he saw that they were moving around the planet, just as the Moon moves around Earth. The discovery of Jupiter's four largest moons was important because it disproved one of the core beliefs held by most thinkers at that time. They thought that every heavenly body moved around Earth. But Galileo's telescope showed that this was not the case. Earth was *not* the center of all things.

Other Early Pioneers

The century that followed witnessed more important discoveries as other scientists built refracting telescopes and trained them on the night sky. In 1655 Dutch astronomer Christiaan Huygens built a scope with a 2-inch-wide (5cm) objective lens. With this instrument, which magnified 50 times, he discovered Titan, the largest of Saturn's many moons. Huygens also observed and correctly identified Saturn's huge ring system.

Another early pioneer, Italian scientist Giovanni Cassini, made some even more spectacular discoveries. Cassini was fortunate to benefit from the work of an Italian lens maker named Giuseppe Campani. Campani and Cassini built the finest telescopes to date. And with them Cassini found four

A satellite named after Christiaan Huygens, who first identified Saturn's rings, took this image of the planet in 2004.

more of Saturn's moons. He also observed cloud bands and other features on Jupiter, determined the length of the day on Mars, and charted the Moon's surface.

Huygens, Cassini, and other researchers also pointed their telescopes at the Milky Way, a misty band of light faintly visible in the night sky. They found the band to be made up of tens of thousands of stars, each too faint to be seen individually by the unaided eye.

This was a stunning discovery. It meant that the universe was much larger than previously imagined.

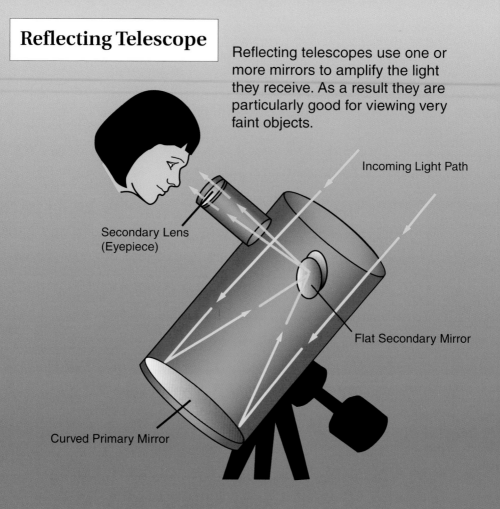

Reflecting Telescope

Reflecting telescopes use one or more mirrors to amplify the light they receive. As a result they are particularly good for viewing very faint objects.

Incoming Light Path

Secondary Lens (Eyepiece)

Flat Secondary Mirror

Curved Primary Mirror

The Invention of the Reflector

Meanwhile, telescopes were not only getting larger and more powerful. The quality of the lenses also improved rapidly, making the images they produced sharper. In addition, some inventors experimented with completely new telescope designs. Among them was a Scottish mathematician named James Gregory. In the 1660s he tried to build a telescope that used a mirror instead of a lens to gather light. But the device was overly complex and did not work very well.

Another researcher soon recognized the potential of this new design. In the late 1600s, English mathematician Isaac Newton, one of the greatest scientists of all time, designed a simpler and better reflecting telescope, or **reflector**. In instruments like Newton's, light enters the telescope's tube from an opening in the front. The light then travels to a mirror located in the back and bounces off. Because the mirror curves inward slightly, the reflected light comes together and forms a small image in the center of the scope. A standard secondary lens then magnifies the image.

As the eighteenth century dawned, a new generation of scientists now had two workable telescope designs. Advances on both soon made Galileo's and Huygen's scopes look puny by comparison. A bright new age of telescopic discovery had begun.

Chapter 2

Expanding the Cosmic Horizon

Ever since Galileo and other early pioneers built the first optical telescopes in the 1600s, astronomers have built larger and larger telescopes. These have required bigger lenses (for refractors) and bigger mirrors (for reflectors). Such large lenses and mirrors are needed because they can gather more light than smaller ones. In fact, the light-gathering power of a telescope is much more important than how much it magnifies objects.

As an example, a reflecting telescope with a mirror one foot (0.3m) in diameter can gather only so much light. So the image produced will have only a certain amount of detail. The telescope's operator may find that this detail looks sharp and clear using an eyepiece (containing the secondary lens) that magnifies 100 times. An eyepiece that magnifies 1,000 times will not reveal more detail. It will only distort the image. To produce an image with more and sharper detail requires a bigger mirror that can gather more light and, with it, more detail.

This is the technical reality that drove astronomers to erect larger optical telescopes in the 1700s, 1800s, and 1900s. With these instruments, they discovered new planets. They also revealed a universe thousands of times larger than anyone had previously expected. Today, the race to build still bigger telescopes continues. Aiding the builders are many examples of advanced technology, including computers.

An early telescope pioneer, Johannes Hevelius, studies the Moon in this illustration.

Formidable Problems to Overcome

In the early years of the telescope-building race, however, the available technology was crude. So the challenges were daunting. One serious problem with lenses for refractors has to do with light. Ordinary white light is composed of a combination of many colors. These colors become visible when rain droplets refract sunlight, producing a rainbow. Early telescope lenses did basically the same thing. As light passed through a lens, it bent, creating the desired image. But the light also partially broke down into its different colors, producing a fuzzy halo of colors around the image.

Between 1733 and 1757, two English astronomers —Chester M. Hall and John Dolland—overcame this problem. They designed a new objective lens that combined two elements. The first was a standard lens, which partially broke light into colors. Directly behind the first lens they placed a second one. The second lens was specially shaped so that it forced the colors to recombine, eliminating the pesky colored halo.

But astronomers soon encountered a second problem with big lenses. These lenses were made

To create large modern telescopes like this one, astronomers had to overcome many technical problems.

of glass. And when the glass was still in liquid form, bubbles and streaks tended to form in it. Such impurities in a lens badly distorted the images created by light passing through it. In 1805 a Swiss craftsman named Pierre Guinand perfected a way of eliminating the bubbles and streaks.

Now astronomers could make lenses considerably larger than any produced before. In 1820 a refracting telescope with an objective lens 9.5 inches (25cm) across began operating in the Baltic republic of Estonia. Several more big refractors followed. Largest of all was the one at the Yerkes Observatory in Wisconsin (inaugurated in 1895), with an objective lens 40 inches (102cm) in diameter.

Herschel, Hale, and the Big Reflectors

Refractors were not the only early telescopes with problems. Astronomers encountered technical difficulties with the mirrors of reflectors, too. First, in the 1700s most telescope mirrors were composed of metal (such as copper) that was highly polished. Because large pieces of metal are very heavy, swiveling big reflectors to follow the stars and planets as they move across the night sky was very difficult. Also, copper and other metals tarnish over time. This forced astronomers to repolish the mirrors at least once a year, a process that often ruined them.

These problems did not discourage or deter a German-born English researcher, William Herschel. One of the greatest astronomers of all times, in the late 1700s he built a series of large reflectors. And with one of these instruments he discovered the planet Uranus in 1781. This was a great milestone in science because Uranus was the first new planet revealed since ancient times. (Before, only six planets were known—Mercury, Venus, Earth, Mars, Jupiter, and Saturn.) Herschel went on to build the largest telescope of his day. Finished in 1789, it was a reflector with a mirror 40 inches (102cm) wide.

Herschel's 40-inch reflector was held up by an enormous wooden framework.

First used in 1949, the 200-inch Mt. Palomar reflector was the world's largest telescope for many years.

Many of the problems Herschel and others had found with reflectors were solved in the following century. In 1850 scientists learned to coat glass mirrors with the chemical silver nitrate. This produced a thin, highly reflective surface. Heavy metal mirrors could now be replaced by lighter glass ones. So reflectors could be made larger and maintained easier.

Leading the way toward a new generation of giant reflectors was American astronomer George Ellery Hale. He managed to raise the huge sum needed to build a 60-inch (150 cm) reflector atop Mt. Wilson, in California. This instrument was able to see individual stars in the nearest **galaxy**, Andromeda. (A galaxy is a huge group of stars held together by their mutual gravities. The galaxy in which the Sun and its family reside is the Milky Way.) Later, Hale helped to build a 100-inch (254cm) reflector on Mt. Wilson. With this mighty scope, American astronomer Edwin Hubble measured the distance to the Andromeda galaxy. Hubble also determined that all galaxies are moving away from each other, so that the universe is expanding.

Hale was also the leading figure in the construction of an even bigger reflector. Located atop Mt. Palomar (also in California), it began operating in the late nineteen forties. With a mirror 200 inches (508cm) across, it remained the largest telescope in the world for several decades.

Multiple Mirrors and Computers

For a while, many people were convinced that the size and quality of the Mt. Palomar scope would never be surpassed. But as has always happened, unexpected new ideas and technologies soon developed. Some telescope designers saw that building ever bigger and heavier mirrors was too difficult and expensive. Instead, they opted for combining several smaller mirrors in a single instrument. In theory, the light-gathering power of the combined smaller mirrors would be greater than that of a single giant mirror. This kind of telescope came to be called a **multiple mirror telescope** (MMT).

The first MMT started operating in 1979 at the Whipple Observatory on Mt. Hopkins in Arizona. It had six mirrors, each 72 inches (183cm) in diameter. They were tightly clustered together in such a way that their images met at a central point. To make the six mirrors work together precisely, the builders connected them to a computer, a device that Galileo and Herschel never dreamed of.

In the years that followed, several much larger MMTs were constructed. These include the largest optical telescopes in the world today—the twin W.M. Keck scopes atop Hawaii's Mt. Mauna Kea. The Keck telescopes each have an array containing 36 mirrors. And each mirror is 72 inches (183cm) across. An advanced computer coordinates the mirrors and takes care of any minor distortions in them.

With these magnificent instruments and similar ones on the drawing boards, astronomers hope to keep expanding the **cosmic** horizon. Telescopes have undergone incredible improvements since Galileo's day. Yet much remains unknown about the vast and wondrous universe in which Earth is but a tiny speck.

Exploring the Invisible Realms

Not all telescopes are optical or work by collecting light and focusing it into the human eye. Visible light is only one form of **radiation**, fast-moving waves or particles given off by various objects. Numerous invisible forms of radiation exist, among them radio waves. Some radio waves are artificial, such as those produced by people to transmit music and voices through the air to ordinary radios. But many other radio waves are natural in origin. Planets, stars, and several other cosmic objects emit radio waves, for instance. And some of these waves reach Earth. Devices that collect cosmic radio waves are called **radio telescopes**. These devices allow scientists to see and study cosmic objects that optical telescopes cannot see.

The First Radio Telescopes

Radio telescopes were invented more than three centuries after the first optical ones appeared. This

This photo shows Grote Reber standing beside his radio telescope located in Virginia.

is because no one even knew about radio waves coming from space until 1931. In that year an American engineer, Karl Jansky, discovered them by accident. He was trying to reduce the amount of static in radio broadcasts and realized that some of the waves causing the static came from the sky.

Another American engineer, Grote Reber, was fascinated by Jansky's discovery. To locate and collect cosmic radio waves, Reber built a metal antenna (or "dish") 31 feet (9.4m) across and shaped like a shallow bowl. It was the world's first radio telescope. With this instrument, Reber made a map of the sky that pinpointed the locations of the strongest cosmic radio wave sources.

Over time other researchers saw the potential for using devices like Reber's to study the sky. Radio astronomy began to come into its own in the late 1940s. In 1946 scientists at the University of Manchester in England erected a radio telescope with a dish 218 feet (66m) in diameter. Many other radio telescopes sprouted up around the world in the years that followed, some of them even larger. The biggest of all began operating in 1963. Located in Puerto Rico, the Aricebo Observatory dish is 1,000 feet (305m) across and covers an area of 20 acres (8ha).

Detecting Mysterious Objects

Using these large radio telescopes, astronomers found that many of the radio sources in the sky are stars and galaxies visible in optical telescopes. By studying the radio waves emitted by these objects, they were able to learn more about them. But radio telescopes also revealed numerous objects that are invisible to optical telescopes. For example, in 1963 astronomers discovered a mysterious object located a great distance from the Sun and Earth. They found that the object, which they named 3C 273, gives off both visible light and strong jets of radio waves. In fact, the radiation it emits is hundreds of times greater than that of the entire Milky Way galaxy, which is made up of billions of stars. So even though 3C 273 looks like a star, it clearly is no ordinary star. For that reason, astronomers called it a quasi-stellar ("starlike") object, or **quasar** for short. By 2003 more than 13,000 other quasars had been found.

Black Holes Revealed

Studies of quasars conducted by radio telescopes since the early 1990s have shown that these strange objects are probably connected somehow to **black holes**. Black holes are extremely dense and massive objects that have very strong gravities. Their gravities are so strong, in fact, that even light cannot escape. That is why they are black. Scientists believe that a quasar is a giant burst of energy released when stars and planets are torn to shreds as they are sucked into a large black hole.

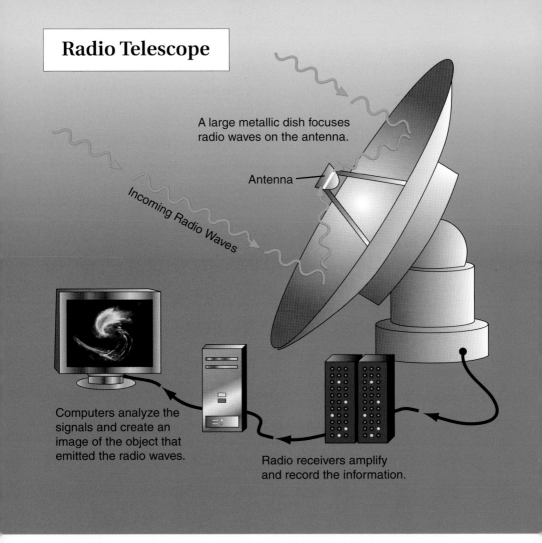

Radio Telescope

A large metallic dish focuses radio waves on the antenna.

Antenna

Incoming Radio Waves

Computers analyze the signals and create an image of the object that emitted the radio waves.

Radio receivers amplify and record the information.

Radio telescopes have also shown that extremely large black holes exist at the centers of most galaxies. This includes our own galaxy, the Milky Way. In the mid-1970s, radio telescopes revealed a very powerful radio source lying in the galaxy's center. They named it Sagittarius A* (pronounced A-star). It was far too energetic and hot to be an ordinary star. In 1997 German radio astronomers showed that thousands of ordinary stars are swirling around

Sagittarius A* at high speeds. It appears to be sucking them in. Astronomers believe it is a black hole possessing the mass of about 3.7 million ordinary stars like the Sun. Radio telescopes have found even bigger black holes in other galaxies, one equal in mass to a whopping 1.2 billion stars!

Echoes of the Universe's Beginning

Another momentous discovery made by radio telescopes was firm evidence for how the universe came to be. In the early years of the twentieth century, some scientists proposed that the universe originated in a gigantic explosion. All known matter was

Two of the more powerful radio sources yet discovered are Quasar 3C 273 (left) and Sagittarius A (right).*

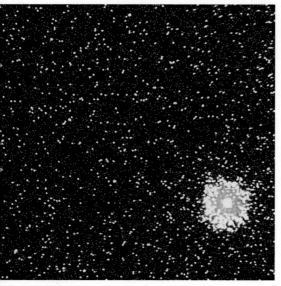 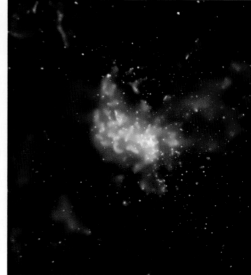

highly compressed into a tiny space. Then it blew apart. As the matter flew outward in all directions, it cooled and became cosmic gases, stars, and planets. This theory came to be known as the **Big Bang**.

For a long time many scientists doubted that the Big Bang had occurred because no direct proof for it had been found. But in 1965 a radio telescope provided that proof. American scientists Arno Penzias and Robert W. Wilson detected an odd form of cosmic radio waves. These were not strong bursts coming from small, centralized sources such as stars or quasars. Rather, the radio waves that Penzias and Wilson observed were faint and scattered evenly throughout the sky.

The two researchers became excited because they realized that only one event could have produced these radio waves. Scientists had long known that an event as violent as the Big Bang would have released huge amounts of radiation. That radiation would have moved outward as the universe expanded, growing fainter over time. And some of it would still be around as a sort of "fingerprint" of the great explosion. Using a radio telescope, Penzias and Wilson had discovered the fingerprint of the big bang.

Searching for ETs

Still another important use for radio telescopes is to search for life that might exist beyond Earth. (Scientists call such alien life **extraterrestrial** and

SETI scientists use powerful radio telescopes like these in their search for extraterrestrial intelligence.

often refer to possible extraterrestrials as **ETs** for short.) This cosmic quest was inspired by a scientific paper published in 1959 by Italian astronomer Giuseppe Cocconi and American scientist Philip Morrison. They proposed that radio telescopes be used to detect artificial signals created by possible extraterrestrial civilizations.

A number of scientists agreed with Cocconi and Morrison and **SETI** was born. SETI stands for the Search for Extraterrestrial Intelligence. Only a year later (1960), astronomer Frank Drake launched Project Ozma, which used the large radio telescope at the National Radio Astronomy Observatory in West Virginia. Drake studied two nearby stars but found no artificial signals. Full-time searches for extraterrestrial signals began in the early 1980s with the opening of the SETI Institute in southern California. The main funding for the project comes from **NASA** (America's official space agency). And SETI presently employs more than 130 scientists.

So far, SETI has studied thousands of stars, most of them located in the section of the Milky Way that contains the Sun and Earth. No alien signals or other evidence for ETs have yet been detected. But the scientists involved in the project are not discouraged. They point out that only a tiny fraction of stars in the Milky Way—less than one-tenth of 1 percent—have been investigated so far. So it may well take several centuries to find any ETs, if they do indeed exist. In this and other ways, radio telescopes continue to reveal the wonders of the universe and humanity's place within it.

Telescopes in Orbit and Beyond

Astronomers sometimes compare human beings to fish. Imagine that some super-smart fish grow hands and build a civilization at the bottom of the Pacific Ocean. Among other things, they construct telescopes designed to study human ships floating high above on the ocean's surface. These fish learn that the bigger the scope they use, the closer the ships will appear. However, the fish astronomers also encounter a serious problem. No matter how large their telescopes are, the amount of detail they can see on the ships remains limited. This is because they are observing through thousands of feet of ocean. And all that water distorts any light and visual images that pass through it.

Human astronomers have the very same problem, except that their "ocean" is Earth's atmosphere. Like water, air both absorbs and scatters rays of light that pass through it. For this reason, images of stars, planets, and other cosmic objects seen through ground-based telescopes are never 100 percent sharp. And a given image will reveal only so much detail, no matter how large the telescope's lens or mirror.

In the early years of the twentieth century, a few astronomers began thinking about ways to overcome this limitation imposed by the atmosphere. The most obvious way, they realized, would be to have a telescope that operates above the atmosphere. No one knows who thought of the idea first. But in 1923, a German named Hermann Oberth became the first scientist to discuss it publicly.

In the years that followed, other researchers considered the concept of a space telescope. One of them was Lyman Spitzer, a scientist at Princeton University, who published an article on the subject in 1946. Spitzer listed some of the potential benefits of an orbiting telescope. It might reveal many

A ground-based image of Uranus (left) reveals less detail than one taken by the Hubble Space Telescope (right).

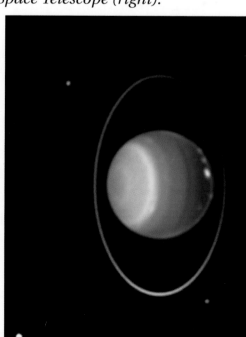

previously unknown cosmic wonders, he said. And it might allow astronomers to see to the very edges of the known universe. At the time, however, few people took the idea of a space telescope seriously. In those days even most scientists thought that space travel was either impossible or would not happen for a century or more.

The Hubble Space Telescope

These attitudes changed dramatically only a few years later. In 1957 the Soviet Union launched *Sputnik*, the first artificial satellite. And before long the United States and Soviet Union were locked in the so-called space race to see which nation would be first to land people on the Moon.

Among the many scientists who were excited about the space race was Lyman Spitzer. In 1962 he met with NASA officials and recommended that they begin planning a space telescope. They agreed that such an instrument was a worthwhile goal. But for various reasons NASA did not launch the project in earnest until 1973, when work on the basic design began. The U.S. Congress approved the funding necessary to complete the telescope in 1977. By that time NASA officials had decided to name the instrument after American astronomer Edwin Hubble, who had pioneered the idea of the expanding universe.

The single most expensive and difficult stage in building the Hubble Space Telescope (HST) was

This photo shows space telescope pioneer Lyman Spitzer in 1948.

preparing the instrument's mirror. (The HST is a reflector.) The main element of the mirror was a glass disk 8 feet (2.4m) in diameter. It had to be carefully shaped and polished, tasks that were accomplished with the aid of lasers and computers. The polishing alone took nearly a year to complete.

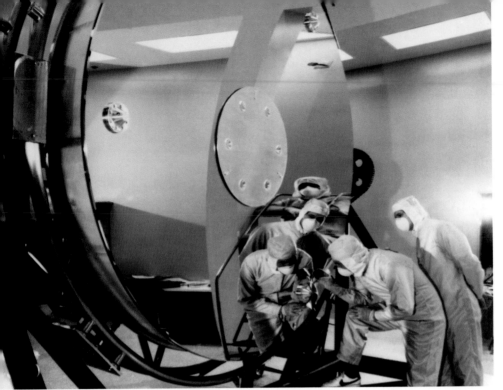

Engineers examine the HST's primary mirror shortly before assembling the telescope.

NASA finally launched Hubble into space in April 1990. It went into orbit around Earth at a height of 375 miles (603km). Powered by solar panels (which transform sunlight into energy), the telescope began capturing images of the universe. At first, the scientists in charge of the mission were sorely disappointed because an unexpected mechanical problem made many of the images look fuzzy. Fortunately, NASA soon overcame this difficulty. In 1993 astronauts from a space shuttle performed a space walk in which they floated to Hubble and repaired its mirror.

Accomplishments of the HST

After the repairs were completed, the space telescope produced results that were nothing less than spectacular. It snapped photos of thousands of galaxies too distant and faint for ground-based telescopes to detect. In revealing these galaxies, Hubble acted as a sort of time machine that could see into the past. This is because light travels at a set speed of 186,000 miles (299, 274km) per second. These galaxies are so far away that the light Hubble captured left them more than a billion years ago. Incredibly, that means that humans are seeing these objects not as they are, but as they appeared in the distant past. In this way, astronomers hope to use the HST to see events that occurred when the universe was very young.

The space telescope's other achievements have been no less exciting. Hubble provided data that proved that black holes are real objects. It helped astronomers confirm that quasars are bursts of energy given off by matter spiraling into giant black holes. And it revealed large clouds of gas, rocks, and debris orbiting a number of stars. Scientists believe that planets are forming in these clouds. In addition, the HST snapped some stunning photos of Comet Shoemaker-Levy 9 smashing into Jupiter in 1994. (The giant gaseous planet was able to absorb the hit without any permanent damage. If the comet had struck Earth instead, human civilization would have been destroyed.)

Hubble's Discoveries

The Hubble Space Telescope is the first telescope to observe space from beyond Earth's atmosphere. Since its launch in 1990, Hubble has sent back thousands of amazing images of our solar system and the universe beyond.

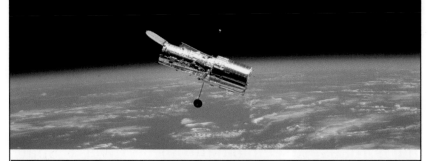

Black Hole
An orbiting disk of dust circles a giant black hole.

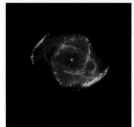

Cat's Eye Nebula
Expanding gas clouds float outward from a dying star.

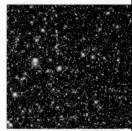

Milky Way
Millions of stars sparkle at the center of our galaxy.

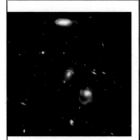

Deep Space
Several galaxies inhabit this patch of deep space.

Molecular Cloud
New stars are born in a cloud of hydrogen gas and dust.

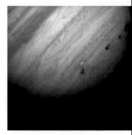

Jupiter
Dark spots mark where Comet Shoemaker-Levy 9 hit the planet.

Future Space Telescopes

The HST is not the only telescope in orbit around Earth. In August 2003 NASA launched the Spitzer Space Telescope. It was named to honor Lyman Spitzer, whose foresight and actions helped make space telescopes a reality. Unlike Hubble, the Spitzer scope is not designed to capture ordinary visible light. Instead, Spitzer "sees" cosmic objects by detecting the heat they give off.

Scientists plan to launch more space telescopes in the future. The first in this new generation of cosmic spyglasses will be the James Webb Space Telescope (JWST), named for a former NASA official. It is presently scheduled to begin operating in 2011. The scope will have a mirror 21 feet (6.5m) across and will float in space at a distance of 940,000 miles (1.5 million km) from Earth. Designers of the JWST hope it will reveal what the universe looked like shortly after the Big Bang.

Some astronomers are also thinking ahead to the day when humans colonize the Moon. They point out that Earth's natural satellite would be an ideal spot for a large telescope. First, the Moon has no atmosphere. So images seen or photographed by lunar telescopes would be razor sharp and very detailed. Also, the Moon has far less gravity than Earth, so everything weighs less on the Moon. This will make assembling and operating giant telescopes a good deal easier than it is on Earth. Optical

An optical telescope took the image of a gas cloud at left. The other image shows the cloud as seen by the Spitzer Space Telescope.

instruments with mirrors hundreds or even thousands of feet in diameter might be possible.

With telescopes like these, future astronomers will be able to see Earth-like planets orbiting distant stars. They will also be able to peer far into the past. Indeed, they may even witness the very beginnings of space and time. If so, a device that began as a plaything of the idle rich will become a key with which humanity will unlock the universe's last secrets.

astronomer: A scientist who studies the planets, stars, and other objects beyond Earth; this scientific discipline is known as astronomy.

Big Bang: The giant explosion in which the universe was born.

black holes: Cosmic objects (often created when large stars collapse) that are extremely dense and have gravity so strong that not even light can escape.

cosmic: Having to do with things beyond Earth or in outer space.

ETs: A popular shorthand expression for extraterrestrial beings.

extraterrestrial: Originating or existing beyond Earth; or a living thing existing beyond Earth.

galaxy: A gigantic group of stars held together by their mutual gravities. Our galaxy is called the Milky Way.

multiple mirror telescope (MMT): A telescope consisting of several mirrors clustered together and coordinated by a computer.

NASA: The National Aeronautics and Space Administration, the official U.S. government agency in charge of learning about and exploring the universe.

planets: Large, spherical objects that usually orbit stars and shine by reflected, rather than their own, light.

quasar (short for "quasi-stellar" object): A cosmic object that looks like a star but emits thousands or millions of times more energy than a star.

radiation: Waves and particles given off by various objects; some radiation, such as light, is visible to the human eye, but most radiation is invisible.

radio telescopes: Large, bowl-shaped antennae designed to collect radio waves and other kinds of electromagnetic radiation.

reflector (or reflecting telescope): A telescope in which a mirror gathers light and bounces it, forming an image that is then magnified by a lens.

refractor (or refracting telescope): A telescope in which a main (or objective) lens gathers and focuses light, forming an image that is then magnified by a smaller lens.

SETI: The Search for Extraterrestrial Intelligence; a group of programs organized to seek out signals from alien civilizations.

stars: Large heavenly bodies that shine by their own light as a result of continuous nuclear reactions taking place in their centers.

universe: The sum total of all the space and matter known to exist.

ziggurats: Towers used by priests in the ancient Middle East as observatories to study the heavens.

Books

Richard Berry, *How to Build Your Own Telescope.* Windsor, CT: Tide-Mark, 2001. Considered by many experts to be the best available general guide for people who desire to build their own telescopes.

Guy Consolmagno et al., *Turn Left at Orion: A Hundred Night Sky Objects to See in a Small Telescope.* New York: Cambridge University Press, 2000. An updated version of a classic guide to the most popular objects visible in telescopes.

Ronald Florence, *The Perfect Machine: Building the Palomar Telescope.* New York: Perennial, 1995. The fascinating story of the construction and epic discoveries of the famous telescope and observatory that were the world's largest for several decades.

Nigel Henbest, *DK Space Encyclopedia.* London: Dorling Kindersley, 1999. This critically acclaimed book is the best general source available for grade school readers about the wonders of space.

Deborah Hitzeroth, *Telescopes: Searching the Heavens.* San Diego: Lucent, 1991. A good general introduction to the history and uses of telescopes.

Michael White, *Galileo Galilei: Inventor, Astronomer, and Rebel.* San Diego: Blackbirch, 1999. A well-written introductory account of Galileo's achievements, including his pioneering use of telescopes to study the heavens.

Mark Voit, *Hubble Space Telescope: New Views of the Universe.* New York: Harry N. Abrams, 2000. An excellent overview of the HST and how it was built, along with many of its stunning photos of the universe.

Web Sites

Facts About Telescopes (www.meade.com/support/telewrk.html). This site is provided by Meade, one of the most reputable telescope manufacturers. It explains in basic terms (aided by diagrams) how telescopes work and the uses of various accessories (such as eyepieces).

Giant Magellan Telescope (http://helios.astro.lsa.umich.edu/magellan/index.php). An excellent site that provides updates on the construction of this huge instrument, which is set to be completed in 2008 (and to become operational somewhat later).

Space Telescope Science Institute (www.stsci.edu/resources). This site contains numerous links to stories and updates about the Hubble Space Telescope and other major space technology and missions.

W.M. Keck Observatory (www2.keck.hawaii.edu). The home page for a great deal of up-to-date information about what is presently the world's largest ground-based telescope.

Picture Credits

In addition to his acclaimed volumes on ancient civilizations, historian Don Nardo has published several studies of modern scientific discoveries and phenomena. Among these are *The Extinction of the Dinosaurs, Ice Ages, The Solar System, Black Holes*, and a biography of Charles Darwin, who advanced the modern theory of evolution. Mr. Nardo lives with his wife, Christine, in Massachusetts.